THE

AWAKENED

RELATIONSHIP

Transforming upsets and blame

into love and harmony

LANDON CARTER

The Awakened Relationship

Transforming upsets and blame into love and harmony

Marshall & McClintic Publishing
200 Coyote Street #1122, Nevada City, CA 95959
Cover photograph and book production - Margaret Jean Campbell

MarshallMcClinticPublishing.com

Printed in the United States of America
First Edition: September 2014

ISBN-10:0991044622
ISBN-13:978-0-9910446-2-7

TABLE OF CONTENTS

Who looks outside, dreams.
Who looks inside, awakens.

Carl Jung

INTRODUCTION

Welcome to *The Awakened Relationship*, a compilation and sharing of what my wife, Diane, and I have found works in our relationship. Our ideas may not be what you are looking for at this time in your life, but we hope you will at least consider them. They are not a reinforcement of the "Falling in Love Fairy Tale" that most of us were brought up with, but these methods have created a "Happily Ever After" that is better than we could have ever imagined.

My wife Diane and I fell in love "backwards," meaning that we began dealing with the hard issues right from the beginning of our relationship. Because we were fortunate enough to discover the principles we want to share with you, we have been growing deeper in love and more connected ever since.

Most of this has been documented in our book *Falling in Love Backwards, an Unlikely Tale of Happily Ever After*. And most of the methods and techniques we use, I first wrote about in *Living Awake: the Practice of Transforming Everyday Life*. Both of these books are available on Amazon.

My relationship with Diane has allowed me to apply the principles from *Living Awake* in the context of an intimate relationship and to experience the true happiness and satisfaction that is available from having a healthy and successful partnership/marriage.

If any of the following questions fit your circumstances, and you really want to create a relationship that works to your total satisfaction, then perhaps we can help you along your journey. Are you asking yourself?

- It started out so good, how did it get so bad?
- Like the old song, "You've lost that lovin' feeling, and its gone, gone, gone"…How do we get it back?
- Given my past failures I am discouraged. How can I set up my next relationship so that it works?
- Our relationship is OK, but how can we really make it the best that it could be?

I will say at the onset, our method is not for the faint of heart. It takes work and can be uncomfortable at times, especially as you are first practicing the techniques we will recommend. But the results of your efforts will be beyond anything you can imagine. At least that is how it has been for us, and continues to be, as we gradually move to deeper and deeper states of connection.

Do you have a good chance of staying together?

If you are already a couple, here are some basic questions you might ask to see if you have a good chance of being successful using our methodology.

Answers to at least two of the three questions should be positive.
1. Do you have common shared core values: spiritual orientation, general political views and common interests?
2. Do you enjoy being around each other, doing things together?
3. Is there, or was there, good physical chemistry/sexual attraction between you?

It is possible to learn and establish new ways of being in any one of these three areas, but if more than two answers are "no," perhaps you should learn the lessons available from your relationship history and work towards creating an amicable exit strategy. Of course, you may find that having cleared up all those old upsets, you are back in love and want to stay together. Either is a possibility.

There is much to learn from your relationship because many of your unhealed wounds will have surfaced in the form of the upsets that drove you apart. These upsets and patterns of behavior will follow you into your next relationship if you do not heal them. So before moving on, if you are willing to get some relationship coaching, you will be much more prepared for the next relationship, more free to be yourself and clearer on what type of person is a good fit for you.

The difference between what normally transpires in relationships and what we are experiencing and recommend.

I won't go into all the variations because that is what makes the story lines for the plethora of popular romantic novels, movies and tabloids. Although most are unrealistic, their popularity speaks to the deep desire we all have for true love, acceptance and connection.

But here is one example: You see someone across the room and there is a strong feeling of attraction. After a short interaction, you are infatuated, high on love, feeling this longing to see the other person. Smitten. Now at this point, in actual fact, you do not know the other person very well, so a major part of what you are falling in love with is your own fantasy about him/her.

He or she appears to be a person who can fulfill that fantasy, who accepts you for who you are, or at least seems to, is interested in you and what you do, and makes you feel happy. The world is brighter, things are better, because he or she is in your life. This high can last for months or even years and is a wonderful feeling; anyone who has had it should feel fortunate. It is what the poets write about.

However, the reality is that each person enters a relationship with a whole list of unexamined expectations. These are mostly not talked about and are based on childhood conditioning (or how your parents acted which you liked or disliked), romantic movies and other fairy tales. Your new partner is supposed to read your mind and know what you need and want. This will lead to one of the components of an upset: unfulfilled expectations.

The next problem comes from the very fact that initially being around this person "made" you happy. So now, when the euphoria ends, and it always does, your mind naturally says, "it is the other person's fault."

Usually we are attracted to people with similar needs and insecurities, but with compensating personalities. For example, I am feeling somewhat insecure, so I marry a person who is successful. But the source of that person's success is his own insecurity that makes him a workaholic. So after the honeymoon, he is not available to pay attention to me.

I have gotten the attention I needed by being a caregiver and therefore take care of my husband, almost like a doting mother. But now my needs are not getting met, I am unhappy, and he is to blame. At this point the arguments, the fights, the withdrawal and the drama begin!

The drama ensues as various patterns and old wounds get reactivated. After some of the emotions have been discharged, reactivating more hurt and pain, there usually is a period of making up, once again trying to reestablish the original connection that has been broken.

This together, apart, together, apart becomes the normal cycle. The usual fix has something to do with the other person changing his or her behavior to stop the upset and make me happy again. This ultimately doesn't work, since it never gets to the cause of the suffering, which are the unhealed wounds within each person. This "changing the other person" fix is trying to "solve the problem at the wrong level."

What we experience and what we are recommending:

My wife and I do get upset and we do experience times when we don't feel connected and even times when we feel annoyed or angry with each other. But we don't argue or blame each other for the way we feel and the upset is over within minutes, with no residue. Being upset or feeling disconnected is our "wake up call" to sit down and examine what is going on for each of us.

We know that if we can get to the bottom of why we are upset that we will be freer to be ourselves. We will be more able to generate happiness and to be the kind of loving person we are each committed to being. And we will end up with a deeper sense of trust and acceptance in our relationship. So for us, upsets are a doorway to a better life experience and are welcomed, even though they can be uncomfortable and unsettling.

The benefits, for us, have been mind blowing to say the least. They show up in our lovemaking, the true test of our connection. We experience times of joyous ecstasy, with long moments of mindless connection with no thoughts whatsoever. Afterwards, we can't even put it into words or in fact even remember, except to say, "that was the best yet." It is as if I am meeting myself, who is my partner, in that 'boundary–less' place beyond time and form.

Also, over time, as we have become more sensitive to each other, that closeness allows more subtle patterns to be noticed and addressed. We realize that all of our programming and patterns will probably manifest within the relationship and that if we continue to operate the way we do, the relationship becomes the ideal vehicle for achieving our personal goal of evolving consciously.

REQUIREMENTS FROM YOU

*"One does not become enlightened by imagining figures of light,
but by making the darkness conscious."*

Carl Jung

An essential life orientation or purpose that will make this method work.

You have a life purpose that roughly could be defined as wanting one or more of the following:

1. To be free from past traumas and childhood conditioning versus being comfortable or right about your view.
2. To consciously evolve into the most refined, loving, powerful, joyous person you could be.
3. To live from an enlightened state of being.

Without this orientation, the work involved is just too uncomfortable, upsetting and painful. You will not want to get out of your comfort zone, or upset the apple cart, to bring up the subjects that you know will reactivate your partner. "Why hurt someone you love? Why embarrass yourself and lower your partner's opinion of you? It will only make matters worse. Better to let sleeping dogs lie. If we just don't talk about those things, the relationship is satisfying enough and certainly better than most," are the mental justifications characterizing most relationships.

But if you have yearned for enlightenment, or to be the best person you could be, or wanted to have the best relationship you could possibly have, then setting your relationship up with the agreements we will recommend and using the techniques we suggest, could be your path to those possibilities. It has been for us.

A word about the goal of freedom: The Hindu and Jain traditions call freedom, "moksha," the release from the cycle of rebirth impelled by the law of karma, the transcendent state attained by this liberation.

Rather than being a remote and unattainable goal, I believe this state is attainable and available to us Now, in this present moment, as the freedom or liberation from the reactivity of the mind. In this awakened state, you have a mind, but your thoughts do not run you and in the process of withdrawing your life energy from those thoughts, and seeing them for what they are, "programming that you are no longer in agreement with," you are free to be yourself. You can show up in the present moment as you choose to BE, no longer repeating your past in an endless loop of karma.

An example from my own life: For those of you who have read Diane's and my book, *Falling in Love Backwards: an Unlikely Tale of Happily Ever After*, you will know that I have been plagued by an attraction to beautiful women. Not just that I would enjoy looking at them, but there was some pull towards them, (some attraction, some attachment) depending on whether I was in a relationship or not, and/or depending on how the relationship was getting along.

If I was out of a relationship, then I took this attraction as a sign from the universe that I should follow it, my standard: "I saw her across the room and fell in love." If I was in a relationship, it might indicate to me that I had something to work on or even make me question the relationship itself.

After much examination of this attraction and recognizing the programming I have been subjected to by our society, I can finally say it is possible to be free of it. While I still recognize a beautiful woman according to society's current standards of beauty, I am no longer pulled by the recognition. It just doesn't mean anything to me anymore. It is more like looking at a beautiful sunset or a piece of art. I am so happy with the reality of Diane's and my relationship that my mind is giving up the struggle that what I have isn't it. This is such a relief!

And another surprising side benefit is that I find Diane more and more beautiful, which gives us both a lot of pleasure.

The essential operating orientation for this method to work.

The orientation that leads to freedom from upsets and a more powerful stance in the world is: I am creating my reality.

This orientation starts at the most central point of the experiential bubble you live within, your own internal experience: your body sensations, thoughts, beliefs, moods, emotions, and images from the past. From here, you can begin to inquire into how these aspects of your experience affect you, and then through your words and actions, how the people and the world around you "show up."

So this is the basic starting point:

1. I am responsible for my experience, for my upsets, and for the reality I am creating.
2. Each person in the relationship is 100% responsible. There are no victims.

I would like to clarify the use of the word "victim." I am not making a judgment against people who feel victimized or condoning any kind of abuse, physical or otherwise. I am only relating this discussion to the necessary orientation for setting up your relationship along the lines that we recommend.

If you try to solve an upset by changing the circumstances or trying to change the other person, as in, "Don't ever do that to me again," then you are **trying to solve the problem at the wrong level**— at the level of the external environment, rather than where the upset resides and originated—inside yourself.

So when you are upset, the first move is to stop, breathe, and to start to observe the nature of the upset. "What am I feeling? When was an earlier time when I had similar feelings? Where does this upset originate?" These are the types of questions that will unlock the upset and begin to create healing. Because you are not blaming your partner, this approach will open up a whole new level of connection, relaxed intimacy and trust between you. It will also lead to more freedom to be your Self.

I always find that my first reaction when I am upset in Diane's and my relationship is, "Diane should change." I don't have to even be very upset, just a little annoyed, like when my blood sugar is low (and really I need to eat) and something which normally wouldn't bother me, does.

Here is a laughable example. When I cook and do dishes, I mostly wash things right away after I use them or if I need a fork, I will wash the dirty fork I just used and then reuse it. Diane just gets another fork out of the drawer and ends up with multiple forks to be washed, often by me, when she does the cooking.

I resisted saying anything about it for a while, as I knew that it was SOOOO petty! But then I finally broached the subject and we talked about it. We have plenty of forks and of course it turns out that it is more efficient to wash all the forks at once and it also saves water. So I am now changing my ways and using more forks!

However, I was actually annoyed and if I had suppressed it, I would have started to lose the authentic transparency, which is the foundation of our relationship. My annoyance stemmed from a misguided desire for efficiency and not wasting things as in "why don't you use just one fork like me?" At least that is how my adult mind justified being "legitimately" upset.

As Diane tends to be tidier than I am, I could not complain about orderliness or cleanliness. I knew the upset linked back to some programming of mine, some way it "should" be, and like a child, I was internally throwing a mild tantrum because reality (what Diane did) didn't fit my picture of how it should be. So I started looking into where the programming originated.

First I noticed the upset had a "This isn't it or this isn't how it should be" element to it and of course I felt like a "victim" of all those forks in the sink! I traced it back to an early incident where I felt out of control and helpless in the midst of life's chaos and then was punished for being messy. Later, I compensated by having everything in order and not wanting anyone to touch my stuff. These memories and feelings all surfaced, as I looked deeper.

Seeing where the annoyance came from and recognizing my own faulty thinking, I was able to easily let it go. And now we joke that Diane's major fault is that she uses too many forks!

"Everything that irritates us about others
can lead us to an understanding of ourselves."
Carl Jung

ESSENTIAL UNDERSTANDINGS

Models that may help in understanding your situation, but more importantly, may empower you to do something about it.

The following models and understandings are covered extensively in my book *Living Awake,* so I will only reference the main points of each. If you do not understand them fully, please read *Living Awake* chapters two and three. One reminder, these models are not necessarily the truth, but like any map, if they get you where you want to go, they have been useful.

The structure of the mind.

The mind is like a stack of holographic multisensory images that gives us the sense of time, records virtually everything that is happening and stores this information in the form of conscious and unconscious memories. It also relates one thing to another, as in earlier similar experiences, to establish patterns of behaviors, thoughts and emotions that seem to be necessary for the survival of the personality, called "you."

The purpose of the mind: Survival of the ego.

The ego is basically who you consider yourself to be and includes your ideas, beliefs, behaviors, etc. The fundamental emotion of survival is fear and the fundamental response to a threat is fight, flight or freeze. In the human behavioral arena, this fight/flight/ freeze response shows up as making yourself right and others wrong, dominating others or avoiding being dominated, controlling or avoiding being controlled, justifying your view and invalidating others and withdrawing. Also, fight is normally expressed with anger, so anger often covers an underlying fear or hurt that got triggered.

The perceptive mechanism's influence on what you experience.

The survival mechanism dramatically affects what you see, sense and feel. In an attempt to cause the survival of one's beliefs or notions of "how it is," only that evidence which supports those beliefs will register on the conscious screen of your awareness. It is very selective and in many cases leads to totally ignoring data and misinterpreting what is received. So you can't entirely trust the evidence you think you received, since you only see what you already believe is possible, not the reverse. This is particularly telling in an argument when you only see the rightness of your point of view.

The nature of upsets.

Upsets are simply a replay of an earlier similar painful experience that is linked together with other similar experiences to form a pattern of behavior. When you are upset, everything you feel and think, say and do, comes from the earlier original experience. This may include body sensations (a tightness across my chest), feelings, attitudes, thoughts, decisions, etc. The feelings you are experiencing will be the same or similar to those you had as a child (annoyance or anger instead of rage for example). But the words are now those of an adult rather than a child.

When you are upset, you are basically a machine on automatic pilot, governed by the mechanism of the ego-protecting mind. There is no action or decision that can come out of this upset that will dissolve the problem, because all your thoughts come from your past programming.

All upsets have, as their nature, being out of present time. You are unconsciously putting your life energy through some programmed pattern. Also upsets (a product of your ego-mind) are telling you, "I don't like the way it is right now. It should be different if he/she loves me. I don't like what he or she is doing or what he or she did. If he

20

or she changes I will be happier. I want something different." So the very nature of upsets is "This isn't it."

Now if you are not upset and want something to change, you take some action, from a neutral position, to change the circumstances. But in an upset, you find yourself a victim of your own programming and it almost always looks like you are a victim of the circumstance or the other person's actions. So there has to be both the "This isn't it" and "I feel like a victim" for it to be an upset.

Of course, we don't want to admit even to ourselves that we feel like victims, but it is the starting point toward freedom, as I mentioned. And it is "the way it is" right now, so don't resist it, work with your upsets and they will become a welcomed doorway to your becoming a more refined and evolved human Being.

An example from my life: Diane and I were shopping for a couch in IKEA. I entered the store without paying much attention to the store layout on the information board as we entered, as the couch section was fairly near the entrance. After not seeing what we wanted and wandering for a while from display room to display room along this programmed path through their giant store, I was ready to leave. I mostly dislike shopping anyway. My motto is "get in and get out."

I started looking for the exit, but couldn't find one. Then we seemed to circle back past the same displays we had seen and still there was no obvious way out. To top it all off, the signs seemed confusing.

About this time, I started to feel angry and trapped, with a tension in my chest and a sense of panic. I was a victim in their planned maze, not in control and I hated it. As there were no store personnel around to help, I started to raise my voice, "How the f... do I get out of here?" Diane who is my angel, and did not make me wrong for being so angry, said, "Take a deep breath Landon, this doesn't seem like you." She brought me back into present time with her words and I followed her advice and started to calm down. She then found a store person and we found our way out. My immediate comment was, "I am never going to IKEA again."

Later as we were debriefing the incident in the car, I realized that the feeling of being trapped, in a maze, and out of control, all

21

seemed to take me back to being born into a world of chaos and confusion. I also saw that I could have taken more responsibility for knowing the store layout, and of course have taken a breath and asked someone how to get out quickly–all without being upset.

But at the time, my unhealed past got triggered, which in turn allowed me to look at it and see it for what it was–a baby's confusion, anger and helplessness at being born into a world which "couldn't be it." The original, "This isn't it."

The other important aspect to note is that it was much easier for me to calm down and let go of the upset because Diane was with me and she was not upset. Often with couples, both people are upset and this makes it more difficult to wake up, stop the drama, and start to observe what is going on in a responsible way.

Later, I also saw that IKEA had done a masterful job of marketing, as I was forced to see so many things that I wasn't looking for. So now when I think, "Where will we get the sinks for the new studio, I think IKEA."

We did go back and bought two couches that were exactly what we wanted and at the best price. I was happy and relaxed that time!

The power of declarations:

We create our personal reality, the "who I am" part of it, through declarations, by stating, "I am … (some way of being)." Before the declaration, there was nothing, after the declaration something exists. You are a god in your own personal experience with the power to create and how you create is through declarations.

These are sometimes in the form of decisions made during physically or emotionally painful events and sometimes in the form of beliefs you unconsciously accepted as a child growing up. We live in this sea of language and dialogue, both internal and external. Some of it serves us, some of it doesn't.

We are all burdened by the unconscious process through which we entered this life and one of our tasks is to become conscious of what we were previously unconscious about, so as to finally take control of our own lives. It happens like this.

In the course of being born into the "already existent conversation" (think beliefs, normative behaviors, attitudes, prejudices, etc. of your parents and the society of your birth), you unconsciously pick up and agree with much of that conversation. After all, how else are you going to survive except by fitting in?

These beliefs, etc. then becomes the unexamined context and content for your life. Your childhood conditioning dictates your personality, values, actions and behaviors, unless you consciously do something about it.

Upsets are just a part of that conditioning, coming up to be repeated and played out in your current life. When you are upset, it is an opportunity to heal that part of your past.

Two critical mistakes:

Two declarative mistakes we all seemed to make in our formative years, starting with our birth, have a huge impact throughout our lives. The first is "I am separate," which brings with it fear of abandonment and rejection, terror of being left alone, anger at being left and a whole raft of strategies to overcome this condition we have unconsciously put ourselves in.

The second is "I am Not Okay" in some form or other. Mine is, "I am not good enough." Everyone has his/her own version of this one. "I am unlovable, bad, flawed, undeserving, invisible, unworthy"– you fill in the blank!

None of these ways of being will get us the love, nurturing and connection we want, so we have all put in place a personality that proves we are just the opposite. For example, "I am an achiever, doing more than expected, excelling, being better than others." Who would suspect that underneath it all, I feel "not good enough?"

So our **structure as human beings** is:
- Who I really am, the Being (perhaps best represented in "form" as the Observer Self, and more accurately as the aware space within which all else arises and passes away).
- Then Who I am afraid I am, the separate, not OK, made up self at the core of our identity.

- Then the false Ego self surrounding that core, pretending and constantly trying to prove that I am Ok, right about my views and better than others, in order to get the love and attention I crave.

It is important to remember this structure because it is the "separate, not Okay self" that usually gets triggered (reactivated) and it is the "who I am pretending to be ego" that rushes to the attack/defense. In the middle of an upset, knowing this structure and where to look will make all the difference.

Diane's Groundhog Birthday, November 2012, Kauai

We were vacationing on Kauai, it was Diane's birthday and it was not going well. I was out of sorts and grumpy, hadn't gotten a card or bought a present or flowers and we were not scheduled to go out to a nice restaurant for dinner. Diane was disappointed because her birthday wasn't meeting her expectations and her unhappiness further exacerbated my feelings of not being good enough. I was feeling depressed and Diane was upset. So we started talking.

It turned out that earlier at the beach at about the same moment that I had judged Diane's body unfavorably when she was running, Diane was feeling insecure about her body. I think these mutual upsets arise simultaneously, as it is difficult to determine if I had the thought first and Diane picked it up and reacted to it or whether Diane was feeling insecure and I picked that up and had the judgment.

I hadn't said anything because I was ashamed about having the thought and withdrew. And Diane didn't mention it until we started to explore what was going on. That was the first thing that came out in our discussion as we tried to determine our part of the joint upset.

Then we talked about my lack of doing something special for her birthday other than the vacation itself. I tend to discount birthdays, while Diane makes a big deal out of them, so we were at odds there. Because Diane was upset (feeling ignored and judged), I was feeling guilty and not good enough and somewhat hopeless as to how to rectify the situation.

24

We decided to declare the following day as her birthday and do it more consciously. The next day, I went out and bought a card and a flower and we swam and had fun at the beach. We made love in the afternoon and had a great dinner at a local restaurant–we had a marvelous day and we both agreed it was perfect.

By being able to talk about what was going on for each of us, without blaming the other, and then to let that go without resentment, we were able to declare a "groundhog birthday" and have a wonderful time–the kind of time we both wanted.

For me, this ability to turn a bad situation around has made all the difference, as it gives me permission to make a mistake that unintentionally upsets my partner, without it being an irreconcilable event. And it allows us to learn from our mistakes so that our future can be more conscious and enjoyable.

AGREEMENTS: ESTABLISHING THE FOUNDATION

Setting up your relationship with agreements.

Agreements define the reality of your relationship and give each person a sense of security as to what to expect from each other. The following are the agreements we have found work for us. I will discuss each in turn and then add a further agreement for relationships in transition.

- I agree to tell you the truth of my experience even though it may be uncomfortable for both of us.
- I agree to be open to discussing any subject.
- I agree to hold your views equal to my own.
- I agree to listen to you without interrupting, even if I am upset.
- I agree to be responsible for my own experience.
- I agree to not blame you when I am upset.
- I agree to be responsible for my own happiness and to commit to generating love and happiness over being right or dissatisfied.

Telling the truth: being transparent to each other.

There is an old saying that "the truth shall set you free." Only by telling the raw truth of your experience can you see it for what it is and be able to finally complete that aspect of your past that has been driving your internal experience and external behaviors.

Of course, while the goal is freedom from your past conditioning, the process can be very uncomfortable. It can bring up all kinds of emotions that will need to be acknowledged and dealt with. You might feel ashamed for experiencing what you are experiencing, or embarrassed, or afraid of revealing it. It may also hurt your listener, which can bring up anger, rejection, etc. until it is cleared up between the two of you. But the only way to freedom is "through" the upset.

Diane will say, "There's something I don't want to talk about." That breaks the ice and allows us to begin talking to resolve where we have gotten hooked by our past. So telling the truth takes an enormous amount of courage and involves some risk to the relationship. It is essential that the process be set up in a very safe space with clear agreements in order to be successful.

Also there is the question, "What is the truth?" It is exactly what you experience, stated in "I" or "my" terms: my body sensations, my emotions, my thoughts, and my interpretations. It is not "you did that and it made me feel this" or "you don't love me," which would be my interpretation of what your actions mean to me. The truth would be "when you do that, I have these thoughts or it triggers these feelings."

Tell your truth as it relates to what you are experiencing and know it is just what is true for you at this moment and it may change in the future.

Open to discussing any subject.

Any topic can be brought up. And there is a commitment to an open space of listening, even though one's initial reaction may be defensive. There is an inherent caveat that you are just going to get the other's point of view. No arguments, just an exchange of ideas and seeking a way to resolve what ever issues arise.

Holding each other's views with equal weight to your own.

This reinforces that you are two equal people in the relationship with a different experience base, different ways of looking at the world, and different ways of interpreting the evidence. It will counter the ego's tendency to be "better than or less than" and start to break up the programming from the male dominated, chauvinistic society in which we were raised.

In the heat of a discussion, this is a very important agreement, reinforcing equality while acknowledging the differences. It doesn't mean that I am automatically agreeing to your point of view, just that I get it and am considering it in this dialogue we are having.

Along with most of the other agreements listed, this was one of my wedding vows to Diane, that I would hold her view equal to my own.

Staying in communication, listening even if upset.

This is an agreement to not walk away or retreat from the only channel that has a chance of resolving your issues. It is a commitment to being present and available. It is a commitment to reducing the pain level as soon as possible, while both of you continue to be responsible for your own experience. This doesn't mean that you are saying, "I am willing to have you dump on me or continue to blame me once that has been pointed out." And it doesn't mean that you can't make an agreement to take some alone time or get some outside help in attempting to sort things out.

I am responsible for my own experience.

Since we are mostly dealing with upsets, situations and conditions that we do not want, being responsible means "I am the cause of my own experience and you can hold me to taking responsibility and looking at the situation from the point of view that I am the cause." This is the only useful focus of your inquiry into the workings of your own mind and ego structure. It is also the only path to clearing it up and being free from that pattern and those unwanted thoughts and feelings.

No blame.

This is a natural corollary to being 100% responsible for my own experience.

I am responsible for my own happiness and committed to generating love and happiness over being right and dissatisfied.

This is again a corollary to responsibility, but a good reminder in the heat of an upset, that I am really committed to being happy. If that is not what I am creating in this moment, then I will get off of my position or do whatever it takes to have the happiness to which I am committed.

This agreement will allow your partner to question what you are experiencing and help you wake up to what you are creating. In that moment it might look like they are avoiding their responsibility in the matter at hand, so it is essential to remember, "this is my life I am creating right now and if is not what I want, I better change."

An example of this in our lives is when Diane questions me if I am grumpy. She may say, "are you grumpy?" I then look and see what is going on. Many times I have unconsciously become annoyed or grumpy and haven't realized it. We can talk about it and it all goes away in a few moments. I will share about this pattern later in the handbook.

A further agreement.

For those of you who read *Falling in Love Backwards* you will recall that when Diane first came to New Zealand, I turned away from her thinking "she's not it" and that I had gotten myself over committed by saying "I surrender to loving you" and inviting her to New Zealand. I would not even hug her when she got off the plane after her 24-hour journey. And Diane was stuck in New Zealand with me for the next 19 days!

In her brilliance, Diane invented the "19 day experiment" in which we would be fully committed to being in the relationship 100% during that time period, tell the raw truth to each other, learn what we could, and be able to part friends at the end with no future commitment. We would either be together or more ready for our next relationship.

This handled my mind always evaluating every new piece of evidence as to whether this meant we should be together or not. It allowed me to relax and just experience the reality of being with

Diane (which I had already appreciated and loved) and in the end, it was that reality which won my heart and kept bringing me back.

So making an interim agreement similar to what we did, is a good way to go for it 100% for a short period of time and allows those of us who are afraid of commitment, for whatever reason, to put that fear aside for a time. It is a way of overcoming your own "this isn't it" mind.

Working within your agreements.

Agreements should be based on something that you know about yourself and are confident you have the ability to do, like: "I will always tell you what is going on with me if you ask." This is better than absolutes, which you may fail at from time to time, like: "I will always love you (assuming that means a feeling) or always be here for you."

Agreements are something you can true up to when you either wake up to yourself or are reminded that you are not keeping the agreement. "I promise to take responsibility for my own experience and if I am blaming you, I will stop." That is the kind of agreement that allows for your human fallibility and yet is an agreement you can keep. It will also create a safe space for your partner to remind you, if you are blaming.

An example:

About a year after we married, I noticed I was annoyed and blaming Diane in my mind for things not being how I thought they should be—some little things that I had not even communicated about so that she would know how I might want them.

In the middle of being annoyed and upset, I woke up to myself and asked, "Why am I blaming Diane for reality (the way it is) not fitting my expectations, my pictures?"

When I saw it, I saw how utterly ridiculous it is to first of all be attached to my expectations over the way it is—a sure way of making myself upset. In fact, this is the very nature of an upset, my ego's survival game, to take me away from "Being Here Now" by trying to convince me that "this isn't it." When in fact, of course, "this is it" and always has been it and if I want to be happy, I better get with the way it is!

Then there was the pattern of blaming the only other person around, Diane, for things not working out my way. Diane said my energy was like I was throwing a tantrum. For me, since it was such an old and frequent pattern, I just felt annoyed and withdrew from being in connection with her. When we shared about this incident later that night, I agreed with her that it was a waste of time to be upset and withdraw. I wasn't having any fun and neither was she.

I then gave her permission to really call me on it next time and that even if I was resisting, to keep going and that I would thank her, for I am committed to ending this pattern. This is a real boon for me, to have someone who loves me and who will call me out until I wake up and get off it and come back into the present. Of course this feels to my ego like criticism of the way I am being and elicits hurt, anger and resistance. In these situations, I especially need to remember that the real enemy is my ego, not Diane!

Once again, this seems to have been an early childhood pattern in which I would throw a tantrum to get my way and withdraw from my mother to punish her for not paying attention to me or not giving me what I wanted. Such is the uselessness of my mind in these instances—contributing nothing to my happiness and in fact, blocking it!

SKILLS NEEDED

"Until you make the unconscious conscious,
it will direct your life and you will call it fate."
Carl Jung

There is a set of skills needed to make this method of relating work. As you practice them, you will become more proficient and confident, knowing that if you apply these techniques, you will get the results you want.

Waking up to your self: Being able and willing to see your self in action, awakening the Observer Self, the Neutral Watcher.
This is covered in Chapter One of *Living Awake* and is the most important and absolutely necessary skill to do this work. You must be able to establish a separation between your Self and your ego, which basically includes everything you would think of as 'me' or 'mine'. Your true self is the awake, neutral nothingness that simply observes. Once this separation is established, it is possible to make some choices from that neutral state, but if you are only in your mind/ego, all decisions will be coming right out of the programming.

Communication: the great art of listening.
It has often been said that since you have one mouth and two ears, you should listen twice as much as you talk. Mostly we don't listen in a way that works, so here are the essentials of effective communication.

1. When you sit down to talk, it is important to first BE PRESENT. I accomplish this by noticing my breath in and out, and feeling my feet on the floor or my butt on the chair. This brings me into the present moment. I am Now Here.

2. Next, put your ATTENTION on the other person, looking into his/her eyes, giving the signal, "I am with you."

3. The next element is INTENTION. The intention to deliver your message so the other person gets it. And the intention to fully receive and understand the speaker's message. Again the 100% responsibility rule applies.

4. As the speaker, deliver SHORT BURSTS so that your listener is not overwhelmed.

5. As the listener, LISTEN WITHOUT INTERRUPTING, unless you are confused about what the other person is saying and then only ask clarifying questions.

6. While you are listening, do not think about what your response will be. This can be difficult, especially when the communication is about you, or what you have done, etc., so you have to be awake enough to notice your thoughts and let them go. Otherwise, you are in your head, disagreeing with the person, planning your response and no longer present or listening.

7. ACKNOWLEDGE that you have heard what the speaker said. This can be as simple as, "okay," "I hear that," "thank you," or "I understand." This piece is often left out of communication, but is key to the speaker feeling heard. This can be called "getting it."

8. If you fully "get" the other person's communication, a very interesting phenomenon occurs. The energy goes off the incident and in some cases the entire issue disappears. What normally prevents this from happening is the misguided notion that if you fully get someone's communication you are agreeing to it. You are not. You are getting fully what your partner is experiencing over there in his/her reality. A test for this would be that if someone keeps repeating the same message over and over, you are not getting it fully.

Real communication takes practice and discipline to unlearn old, bad habits, but it is the life-blood of this method of relating, so taking the time to master it will allow you to reap huge benefits.

Welcome rather than resist upsets.

"What you resist persists."
Carl Jung

My wise wife Diane said, "Upsets are the doors to freedom and deeper connection." This orientation turns your life into a fascinating journey of self-discovery and leads you toward your goal of enlightenment and freedom. Releasing conditioning and attachment to your ego identity is the path regardless of the form you choose, whether it is a cave, an ashram, or dervish dancing.

In this case, the form is your relationship and the opportunities for inquiry your relationship presents. It is my notion that this can be one of fastest paths, since being with someone in an intimate relationship will definitely bring up all the old childhood wounds. And for us, the benefit of healing these wounds has lead to deep love, happiness and bliss.

Five steps to handle an upset.
1. Recognize you are upset.
2. Take responsibility; own your upset (no blaming).
3. Forgive others for triggering your upset and yourself for having it.
4. Look and see what the current situation has triggered from your past. "Oh, I'm feeling invisible, just like I felt as a child," for example. Each time you can spot the connection to the past, you are lessening its power over your life and creating more healing and more freedom to be who you choose to be.
5. Choose to not put your life energy through that programmed behavior from your past. Choose some other way of "showing up."

Of course you have to first have an upset and then wake up to the fact that you are upset. This is the "recognize" part. As you progress, you will notice that some of the upsets and dysfunctional programming are pretty subtle. What you once thought was normal, you now see as programmed behavior that you are no longer committed to.

I have noticed this about being a male, in a male chauvinistic society. As more of my grosser upsets dissolve, like my "not good enough" pattern or my "this isn't it" pattern, I am becoming more aware of male tendencies that probably stretch back to cave man days. The more I can access those tendencies, the more freedom I have to choose how I want to be in the world.

Working through upsets.

> *"Man's task is to become conscious of the contents*
> *that press upward from the unconscious."*
> Carl Jung

The key is to see upsets as opportunities (the doorway to deeper connection and more personal freedom) rather than as problems. Then, through the process of observation, start to become fascinated with the workings of your own mind. This is the process of "knowing yourself," both the strengths of your personality and the dysfunctional aspects. Once you know yourself at a certain depth, then you can choose not to direct your life energy through those dysfunctional patterns and can actually choose different ways of Being.

The way you are Being is the causative element in your reality and from it all else manifests. In fact, when you really examine the nature of Time and Being-Here-Now, you will see that the only real choice you have in this present moment is "how am I showing up, how am I Being." You will also notice that your mind is not your friend, since it is not committed to the love and happiness you say you want.

While your mind is not your friend, it can be "befriended" if you realize that when you are upset, your mind is only bringing up issues that are unresolved, unhealed, and incomplete. If you can stay "awake to yourself," keep your Observer turned on, then life's circumstances and your mind will bring up what is next for you to deal with. It will define the path to freedom, your unique path, as each new layer of subtlety gets revealed, observed, and the patterns that bind you are released.

If you can stay awake to yourself, you really become your own guru, your own teacher. But you must stay awake. If you don't, you will be lost in the maze of your own mind and subjected to the tyranny of its programming. When you are awake and detached (coming from the neutral observer) you can make choices about how you want to BE and this will make all the difference in your life.

As you release more and more of your past programming, you will have more space (emptiness) into which you can choose how you want to BE and increasingly those ways of being will become your normal personality, unaffected and unchanged by the types of circumstances that previously used to upset you.

MORE EXAMPLES

"Seldom, or perhaps never, does a marriage develop…smoothly and without crisis; there is no coming to consciousness without pain."
Carl Jung

The following are **examples from our life together** that hopefully give you more reality on the process of working through upsets. Most of these have come from my blog where I have been chronicling my life. The awake life is certainly not lacking in issues to examine and depths to plumb!

Resisting Diane telling me what to do. September 4, 2013 Nevada City
I started noticing this as a pattern only recently. Back in February when we were in New Zealand, Diane was trying to get me to call someone to help with cleaning in preparation for the wedding celebration we were holding at my house in Golden Bay. She asked me several times and I finally did the task reluctantly. But before I complied, I got really angry and yelled in a loud voice for Diane to "Stop telling me what to do!"

It was so out of character for me that she did not react and just thought, "he is really upset, something got triggered." I calmed down, admitted that it was probably me having to comply with my mother's expectations and the anger I had felt in complying. After all, as a child, I really couldn't "not comply" because I was the "goody two shoes" of the family, the older brother, committed to meeting or exceeding all my parent's expectations.

39

The role of the 'moderate rebel' was left to my year younger brother who, to this day, is more creative than I am. So I am sure that I resented at a deep level the lack of freedom that the compliance required.

Then recently, it was just a little thing that Diane suggested, something that would contribute to my well being and I closed down, didn't like her and didn't want to do what she had suggested. She felt she could not contribute to me and was therefore somewhat "invisible" (one of her buttons). I felt "not good enough" and noticed my mind saying, "get off my back, leave me alone, let me do it myself." This time my response was much more subtle, but it still damaged the connection that Diane and I normally maintain.

As we talked about it, I recognized that it related once again to my resisting my mother's expectations and her insistence I be a certain way. Also there was a mandate (stated by my father) to not express anger towards my mother. So I think I had a lot of bottled up suppressed anger. I do remember, that I couldn't get away fast enough to go to boarding school at fourteen. Finally I was on my own!

I had all this conditioning, even though I got lots of support from my mother as I was growing up. In fact, I was extremely fortunate—my own horse, camping and skiing trips, a calm, good family atmosphere, which was safe and loving, if not overly expressive.

It was just these underlying expectations of who we were and how we needed to act in order to get my mother's attention and love that curtailed my sense of being freely myself. And even though I now appreciate my "upbringing," I am left with this anger that is now surfacing in the safety of my loving and authentic relationship with Diane.

In past relationships, this resistance (upset) would have surfaced as a big row. Her side, "You don't love me, because you don't do what I ask." "You don't let me contribute to you." My side, "Get off my back." "Stop nagging me." And of course all the accompanying feelings of anger, resentment, sadness and the pulling away from whatever level of intimacy had preceded the argument.

I am so thankful to have Diane as my partner, so that I can have these uncomfortable and potentially relationship-ruining challenges come up and be able to talk about them and finally let them go. We both recognized recently that whatever patterns are still left will mostly surface and get expressed within our relationship. We are so grateful that we have the tools to deal with them!

Revealing my "This isn't it" pattern. September 18, 2013, Nevada City

Yesterday while I was walking on the way to the garden of our beautiful farm, I noticed I was annoyed and angry, and kind of depressed about life. I could not find a reason for feeling this way, as much as I looked at my life and what might have triggered the upset. As I started to explore the feelings more, I noticed a kind of dark shadow over my life at that moment and my posture was somewhat hunched over.

I thought to myself, "This is crazy, I have what I want. I live where I want to live, I am married to the woman I want to be with, we are comfortable financially, I am rowing competitively and able to row. What is going on?"

Normally I would ignore this feeling and just go through my day with the edge of enthusiasm missing, the satisfaction and joy evaporating. I would get involved in some activity but the shadow would remain, robbing me of the thrill of being alive and tending to make me withdraw from Diane.

Sometimes I would talk myself out of it, consciously looking for beauty, or reminding myself of my good fortune. This time I just observed the dark shadow and the anger and the lack of enthusiasm and my hunched over posture. And all of it disappeared.

I realized that against the backdrop of a life that I love with Diane, my old nemesis of "This isn't it" is revealing itself for the pattern it is. My mind continually wants to sneak in and rob me of joy and make a problem out of our good life. But now I am on to it at a new level, so I expect to see it overshadow my life less and less.

I am blessed with the good fortune to have such a supportive partner, who less and less gets hooked when I am upset and withdrawn and to have a life that I actually want, which becomes a backdrop to reveal these subtle patterns. Even though these upsets are often uncomfortable and "aliveness damaging," I welcome them as I know they are the doorway to more joy and happiness, once I can observe them and they disappear.

41

Winning the Head of the Charles, October 2013, Boston

I have been trying to win the Head of the Charles Rowing Regatta for 15 years since the last time I won in 1997. So I should have been very happy when I won, (and as I write this I am), but at the time I didn't think I had my best race. A number of rowers broke records in other age categories, so I was down on my self for not breaking a record–the mind trying to make me unhappy, taking the win away, and trying to repeat the "I'm not good enough" pattern.

Thankfully Diane was there to say, "Landon, you just won the Head of the Charles, something you've wanted to do the whole time I've known you. Don't let your mind take your win away. Let yourself have it." She was so right.

She would also say when people congratulated me, "Let the acknowledgement in, you won, you did what you set out to do!" I am so grateful to have Diane as my partner, someone who is awake when I am not and with whom I can share my inner mind chatter and feelings. Then together we can look at the machinery of the mind.

Once again, I conclude that my mind is not my friend! Sometimes a tool, sometimes a field where positive thoughts, intentions and feelings are expressed, but not my friend–as in someone I can always count on to tell me the truth.

My Grumpy Addiction. January 2014, Golden Bay, New Zealand

I recently was reviewing my life as an exercise to let go of the past. As part of that process, I was immersed in the fact that I did not have work or a current project that I was inspired to do, which contributed to others and made money. I just barely noticed that I was sad about it. And I was angry that "my life hadn't turned out as I wanted it to" even though I wasn't clear what that "turned out" would have looked like. "Here I was at 70 and my life hadn't worked out, I was a failure!"

Of course this was just another form of "this isn't it," but I was not aware of it at the time. Instead, I was barely aware of the sadness, and afraid to admit that I was angry–something to do with not being allowed to be angry with my mother. So I suppressed the anger, which made me depressed and that manifested as being GRUMPY.

This mood made my life miserable and affected Diane, even though she did not take it personally–thank God! She said I am like a big grumpy bear and she is going to get me a hat that I will have to wear when I am being that way.

This whole pattern is based on an interpretation that just isn't true. It amazes me that I can even entertain such a thought for a moment, but then sleepwalking is hard to overcome after a lifetime of practice! The real truth is that I do have everything I want: health, a great partner, energy, choices, and financial security.

My mind, my ego, is once again trying to sabotage my experience of abundance; to cause its own survival by playing the old "this isn't it" game in a slightly different or more subtle way. If I did really get that I had what I wanted, the game of "my satisfaction will be in the future" would cease to exist. So I need to be constantly on my guard against my own self-defeating, pain and suffering producing, ego. I need to let go of having to DO something to fix something and just BE satisfied.

The scary thing is that while I was feeling grumpy (depressed), I had an interaction with Diane in which she asked a reasonable question and I said (with irritation in my voice), "You're always trying to fix things, even when it's not your problem. Why waste yours and my time?" After which, I felt better! I had released some of the energy, but it was totally misplaced and inappropriate.

Luckily, Diane did not take the bait and start a domestic scene filled with drama. And we had a chance to look at it together shortly thereafter. It seems to me that much of what is argued about in relationships is just the release of suppressed anger from somewhere else, covering sadness or fear.

Grumpy without a cause. June 2014 Nevada City
Diane and I had recently had a blissful date and were happy with each other and our life. We both felt appreciative and thankful.

So why was I Grumpy and Irritated with little things that she did, using too many spoons, not hanging up dish towels, stupid stuff that usually I don't care about?

In looking into the pattern, I have discovered two things. One, I am filled up with everything I want and not used to simply appreciating what I have without wanting something more, or better, or different. For example, setting a new athletic goal, or going on an adventure, or doing something that is fun, like skiing.

And second, I have been entrained in the grumpy pattern physically. It was my way of punishing others for not getting what I wanted. Or it was a reaction to my physical pain, or my not being as good as I used to be when I was younger in things like rowing or skiing. I saw that I was physically grumpy, and emotionally grumpy, and I was desperately looking around for a cause! And I couldn't find a cause because I have what I want. So in this instance there was the grumpiness looking for a justification, caught in the act: grumpy without a cause!

I realize that I now have all this extra time and energy being happy with where I am. I am no longer looking around for who I am going to be with and I am not so interested in just another goal or project to fill the empty space of boredom. And I am unpracticed at appreciating what I have. Such as finding beauty, where I haven't been looking. Or counting my blessings for all the abundance that fills my life.

In the past, irritation and grumpiness have gone hand in hand and I have been reluctant to say I was irritated, since the things I was irritated about were so petty. Now I have enrolled Diane in telling me if she notices me being grumpy and I am committed to getting off it, not being grumpy about her telling me I am grumpy! Such are the benefits of having the relationship we have. I recognize that my grumpiness has robbed us of the pleasure we so often experience together and I am committed to getting rid of that pattern.

FURTHER PRACTICES

Keeping your mind out of your relationship:
Surrendering to reality versus chasing the fantasy.

There are several aspects to this. First, is the actual reality of your experience, both the external and internal physical reality and your emotional state. Then remembering that your perception mechanism distorts what you see and feel according to your internal biases. Finally, knowing that your fantasies show up on the same mental screen as any other thought.

As described in our book Falling in Love Backwards, I always liked the reality of my experience with Diane and that is why I kept coming back. My fantasies, as they surfaced, had to be dealt with, of course, and I was less and then more successful in seeing them for what they were at various stages of our journey. But I always knew that I needed to surrender to reality.

As I fell in love with Diane, I suffered when my perceptions and fantasies didn't match the reality of our past experience, or what I wanted my experience of our relationship to be. In other words, if I was annoyed with Diane, I suffered and I knew it was contrary to what I wanted to experience. I also knew it had everything to do with me and not her, so I would start looking at how I was not living up to my own standards and feeling not good enough, and projecting that onto her.

The second aspect was my ability to discern between the various messages on my mental screen. Is what I am seeing real or fantasy? Is the interpretation that I am giving to what I see necessarily the truth for me? What do I (the Being) want versus what my mind is bringing up? So if I am committed to happiness and to love, what am I doing being angry and blaming my partner? It doesn't mean that the anger immediately disappears; it just means that I know where I am headed.

The bedroom caldron:
Setting aside times to make love.

We like to make love in the afternoon when we can see each other and are not tired, as we would be at the end of the day. Our sequence: We start by looking into each other's eyes and talking about any upsets or times when we have not felt connected. This might take the better part of an hour. We keep talking while we shower together, (outside with our double-headed shower), light some candles (it is a sacred event), turn on some music, and snuggle. After perhaps more talking, we feel really connected and are looking into each other's eyes with fewer and fewer thoughts.

Then there comes a time when we agree to stop talking, as the urgency of thoughts fades into the background and we can let go of any passing thought and be totally present. At this point, we just start to enjoy the pleasure of the physical sensations and the flow of energy throughout our bodies and between us. As we make love, we experience this dance of ecstatic connection, with no boundaries and rarely any thoughts. Afterward, we stay snuggled together, enjoying the after glow of love and gratitude.

Using the bedroom intimacy to get out of your head:
The "dickometer."

From time to time, a thought might come up while we are making love. It can be as subtle as me observing us making love, but nevertheless, it means that I am in my head.

If I can't let the thought go and return to the ecstasy of the physical experience, then usually the energy between us drops and so

46

does my erection. When we have identified the thought, and often we are so attuned at that point that we both had thoughts, then we can let those thoughts go and start again, round two!

I have jokingly said that I have a "dickometer" that is sensitive to whether we are in present time with each other or not. But that has taken us a while to be sensitive enough to what is going on and lots of talking about what is coming up at any time before or during our love making.

In the beginning I would just feel "inadequate" and "not good enough" if I started to lose my erection. And Diane would have a corresponding thought of, "Oh no, he is not interested," so she would hold back some and it would become a self-fulfilling prophecy.

This even led to me resisting us making love, as I was afraid I would not be as good as I was the last time. Therefore Diane would not be satisfied, so why bother going into a situation where I was going to feel inadequate and Diane was going to be disappointed? That took a while for me to get through, but Diane never made me wrong and by talking about it we moved through that "upset."

Enjoying the benefits of all the work.

For us, our lovemaking is where we experience the intensity of our connection. It is that holy place of meeting the other beyond time and form. In a way, it is our personal experience of God and Goddess uniting.

You would think that given how good our lovemaking is for both of us, that we would be like bunnies, never leaving the bedroom! But it is interesting how the activities of each day seem to take us on our own separate paths, still feeling connected, but in a less intense, more usual way. So we schedule the time for our dates and build our calendars around these important events.

Filling your life with what you want.

"I am not what happened to me, I am what I choose to become."
Carl Jung

We have spent most of this handbook describing how to eliminate unwanted and dysfunctional programming so as to become a more refined and evolved human Being. This process of eliminating unwanted aspects of your personality creates the space and emptiness into which you can create through the power of declaration "who you are now Being." For example, "I am an authentic, loving man, committed to being happy and to helping others to be happy."

I have discovered another important element of living an awakened life and that is to fill the emptiness with Gratitude and Appreciation. Before we go to sleep every night, Diane and I cuddle together and say what we are grateful for and then acknowledge each other for something we appreciate about the other from the day. For me, who has been unskilled in appreciating others, this practice has brought some wonderful results.

I am now able to switch into being thankful for all I have, when I notice myself "this isn't it-ing!" I simply remind myself that I am happy living in the reality in which I find myself, married to the woman I love, living where I want to live, doing what I want to do, and having enough resources.

While the shadow of "this isn't it" has plagued me most of my life, this underlying and pervasive upset is fading and when it does surface, I easily shift to gratitude. This has made all the difference for me in the quality of my life.

So my final recommendations are to put in place some practices to remind yourself to be thankful for the aspects of your life that you are thankful for and to verbally appreciate your partner and those around you. Remember, the mind can only focus on one thought at a time. So filling your thoughts with gratitude and appreciation can make all the difference for you as well.

RECOMMENDED PRACTICES FOR COUPLES

The following is a summary of the practices recommended by us as you start to implement this form of relationship.

1. Practice turning on the Observer Self through a simple meditative practice each day. Sit quietly for at least 10 minutes. Close your eyes, feel your feet on the floor and your butt on the chair. Then start to follow your breath, in and out, using a point on your upper lip below your nostrils as the focal point. At first, see if you can count breaths, one to ten, without being distracted by a thought, or following a thought or image, or getting lost in a thought or image.

If you get lost, start again at one. When you get to ten, start again at one. As you start to build the strength of your Observer and are able to stay present and centered in the face of passing thoughts, you can let go of the counting. Then you simply sit and follow your breath. You are developing the ability to Observe your mind in action and not get hooked by it.

2. Take a moment each day to sit opposite of your partner, with one person's knees on outside and the other person's on the inside, so you are relatively close. Then gaze into the other's eyes without talking or trying to communicate in any way. At first you may find it difficult to "BE with your partner" without some reaction, but with a little practice you can let go of all facial expression and simply gaze into each other's eyes.

If you look away, or start to laugh, or react in some other way, see how soon you can return to the exercise. You are working toward being present with your partner and maintaining a totally neutral state of deep presence. This is the basis for all the communication that is to follow–being present with your partner. You should set a timer for 5 minutes or more so as not to be worried about the time.

3. Monitor your moods throughout the day. Notice how you feel about yourself and your partner, what thoughts you have, etc. You may want to jot these experiences down for communication later. It is also interesting to note the time, as often, both of you will have corresponding upsets at the same time. The more you can notice when you are upset, the faster you will be able to let it go.

4. Pick a topic without much charge on it. It can be a challenging topic, but one that is not very big. Practice the communication methodology described on pages 24 and 25 until you feel that each of you has been thoroughly heard by the other. Do not try to solve anything until you can get to that place of neutrality where you are not trying to solve your upset by having the other person change. They may offer to change to become a more conscious and refined human being, but it is not to keep you from being upset. A delicate balance!

5. Formalize your agreements so as to set up the relationship consciously. This will create a safe space for communication and give you something to true up to when you stumble.

6. On more difficult issues, if possible, only explore one side of the issue at a time. What happened that got me hooked? What in me actually got triggered? (Here it will be important to explore your version of "Not OKness" that got reactivated and is supplying all the emotional content. As well as looking at the mechanisms you employ to defend against experiencing those emotions.) This is where the real benefits come, so don't give up. Each time you Observe the pattern and talk about it, the upset gets weaker and you get stronger, so keep looking.

7. When you have together looked at one side of the upset as much as you can in that session, then you can both explore the other side of the upset. For example: she gets angry at something I did, I feel her anger and withdraw. What got triggered was my "not good enough." Then I judge her for something, get irritated, don't like her, strike back, etc. You know your own drama!

8. Schedule times to make love. This includes time for the whole sequence of talking and gradually getting more present with each other. You don't have to actually make love, but you should use the opportunity to come up against any barriers to making love and talk about them. Even this disappointing experience can be satisfying when you realize that whatever the barriers are, they are finite, not infinite, and with enough Observation and talk applied to them, they will disappear. So you are on the path to the relationship you want.

CONCLUSION

We hope that this little handbook assists you in having the relationship of your dreams and furthers your conscious evolution at the same time—a real win/win situation!

I periodically do a course called "Foundations of Mastery" that teaches four necessary conditions for being on the path to mastery: non–resistance, non–reactivity, non–judgment, and non–attachment. I trust that through our sharing in this book you will realize that we all get resistant, reactivated, judge others, and are attached to our views and our identity.

That is the start of the process we are advocating. To begin, we need to accept those experiences within ourselves, be authentic, and admit we are upset, which is, in itself, a form of non-resistance. Then the skill becomes how fast we can let go of those negative experiences and choose another way of being. Welcome to the path of mastery.

If you have any questions or want clarity on any issue, please do not hesitate to contact us. Also feedback about the usefulness of this book, or suggestions on any way it can be improved would be welcomed.

We recognize that knowing what to do and doing it are two different things, so we are available to assist you in implementing any aspect of this material, either through seminars and workshops or with personal or couples coaching.

To contact us, please email me at landon@landoncarter.co.nz or through our website, www.fallinginlovebackwards.com. We can then arrange a call or continue using email to determine what will work for you.

Landon Carter, Nevada City, California, September 2014

A NOTE FROM DIANE

Five years ago, in 2009, Landon's book, *Living Awake*, provided an opportunity for our paths to cross. I had some ideas for him to make his book stronger, include more stories, etc. I am so grateful to that book for opening a door to the powerful and meaningful relationship and life that I now share with Landon.

Our book, *Falling in Love Backwards, an Unlikely Tale of Happily Ever After,* describes the journey we shared, discovering the truth between us and facing our own unhealed pieces of the past. We didn't realize that we were creating a path of stability, joy and deep love. It felt, at times, more like a scary rollercoaster, and one that I wanted to get off, more than once. That's why we say that we fell in love "backwards"–there was no fantasy beginning. Just the tough issues right off the bat.

Now, five years later, we're both so grateful for the Divine Providence that not only brought us together, but also allowed us to persist through all the challenges that we faced.

So we're offering you this handbook in the hope that you can also discover the freedom and love that wait on the other side of the difficult issues that come up in an intimate relationship. As Gay and Katie Hendricks say, you can be "learning allies" together, committed to your own and each others' healing as you share the journey of intimacy.

Wishing you joy and deep and lasting love in your life,
Diane Covington-Carter

www.ingramcontent.com/pod-product-compliance
Lightning Source LLC
Chambersburg PA
CBHW071343290326

41933CB00040B/2153